Guillaume Apollinaire

The Flaneur of Paris

Translated by Alex Andriesse

Hermits United
London · Paris

Published in Great Britain by Hermits United Ltd. 2026

Translated from Guillaume Apollinaire, *Le flâneur des deux rives*
(Éditions de la Sirène, 1918)

English translation © Alex Andriesse 2026

A catalogue record for this book is available from the British Library
ISBN 978-1-916658-14-1

www.hermits-united.com

The Flaneur of Paris

Memory of Auteuil

Men cannot walk away from anything without regret. They cannot even part with the things, people, and places that have made them most miserable without a pang.

So it was in 1912 I left you, not without bitterness, far-flung Auteuil – charming quarter of my deepest sadness. I would not go back until 1916, to be trepanned at the Villa Molière.

When I moved to Auteuil in 1909, rue Raynouard still looked as it had in Balzac's time. It's quite ugly now. There is still rue Berton, lighted by oil lamps, but soon, no doubt, that will change.

Rue Raynouard is an old street on the border between the neighbourhoods of Passy and Auteuil. Were it not for the war, it would have disappeared, or at least become unrecognisable.

The municipality had decided to implement alterations, widening the roadbed and making it suitable for vehicles.

That would have been the end of one of the most picturesque stretches of Paris.

In the beginning the street was a path that climbed from the banks of the Seine, through vineyards, to the hilltops of Passy.

It looks almost the same as it did when Balzac used to scurry down to escape from some tiresome visitor and go catch the Saint-Cloud stagecoach to Paris.

If you walk from the Quai de Passy and glance down rue Berton, all you'll see is a run-down road full of stones and potholes hemmed in by ruinous walls; to the left, the fence of an admirable park; and to the right, a tract of land whose owners have put it to various and very peculiar uses. One part is laid out as a garden with a vegetable patch a stone's throw away. Some bits of architecture remain, and if you walk through the big door on the quai, you go up a wide sandy path up to a big wooden theatre. Not the sort of building you'd expect to find in such a place, it is called the Joan of Arc Playhouse. In 1914, a few ragged posters, ancient even then, informed you that once, perhaps five or six years earlier, *La Passion de Notre Sauveur Jésus-Christ* had been performed there. The actors may have been men and women of the world. You may have run into the Christ of Auteuil in a salon. A converted stock-market baron may have played, perhaps to perfection, the thankless role of the Cainite saint Judas, who got his start in finance, moved on to apostasy, and ended up a sycophant.

But let the walker continue down rue Berton, and he will soon see its side-streets are running over with inscriptions – with *graffiti*, to speak like an antiquarian. Thus you learn that LILI OF AUTEUIL LOVES TOTOR OF POINT DU JOUR and that she marked the fact by drawing a heart pierced with an arrow and the year: 1884. Alas, poor Lili, the years that have passed since your pledge of love must have healed the wound that once stigmatised your heart! Generations of anonymous writers have blazoned all the passion of their souls with this deeply carved cry: LONG LIVE THE LASSES!

Over here is a more tragic exclamation: CURSED BE THE 4TH OF JUNE AND HE WHO WROUGHT IT. And so the blissful or baleful graffiti runs on until, on the left side of the street, it reaches an ancient pile with a superb porte-cochère flanked by two slope-roofed, free-standing houses very near a traffic circle, where an entry gate leads into a marvellous park with a well-known nursing home – and also where you find the only thing connecting, albeit tenuously, the post is so poorly run, rue Berton with Parisian life: a letterbox.

A bit farther up, you come to some rubble loomed over by a big plaster dog. The cast is intact, and I have always seen it in this same spot, where it will probably remain until the diggers come and renovate rue Berton. The street then takes a sharp right turn, but before the bend there is another gate, and behind it a modern villa encased in a cleft in the hillside. It looks miserably new in this old street, which, seen from the bend, flaunts its ancient and unexpected beauty. Now it narrows, a stream trickles down the middle, and over the walls that clutch it tight, leafy branchings spill out from the big garden around Dr Blanche's nursing home – a whole luxuriant vegetation casting its cool shadow over the old road.

Here and there boundary stones have been set against the walls, and above one of them is a marble plaque, stating that here, in former times, was the borderline between the seigneuries of Passy and Auteuil.

Then you come to the back entrance to Balzac's house. The main entrance is in a building on rue Raynouard. You have to go down two stories and – thanks to the kind ministrations of the late Monsieur de Royaumont, the Balzac Museum's curator – you can, if not descend the same staircase that Balzac took to reach rue Berton (that one is sealed up), at least go down another staircase into the courtyard the novelist must have crossed, through the door that led him into rue Berton.

At this point, you reach a place where the street is wider and inhabited. There's a house that backs onto rue Raynouard and juts out over it. A vine has climbed all over the house front, and fuchsias grow in the flowerboxes. Some very steep, narrow stairs lead to rue Raynouard, opposite the new road, the old Avenue Mercédès, today known as Avenue du Colonel-Bonnet, one of the most modern thoroughfares in Paris.

But you're better off continuing down rue Berton as it dies away between hideous walls, behind which there's no vegetation to be seen, until you come to an intersection where the old street runs into rue

Guillou and rue Raynouard, across from an ice factory that shivers day and night with the noise of churning water.

Those who walk down rue Berton when it's at its most beautiful, just before dawn, will hear a harmonious blackbird giving a marvellous concert, accompanied by the music of thousands of other birds, and, before war, the pale flames of a few oil lamps that burned in the old streetlamps – not yet replaced – used to flicker at this hour.

The last time I went down rue Berton before the war was a long time ago, with René Dalize, Lucien Rolmer, and André Dupont, all three of whom have died on the field of honour.

But there are many other charming and curious things in Auteuil...

Even now, between rue Raynouard and rue La Fontaine, there is still a little square so simple and tidy that one cannot imagine seeing anything so pretty anywhere.

In that square is a gate that guards the last Hôtel des Haricots! A name that conjures the Empire and the National Guard. It was there they used to send guardsmen punished for infractions. They were handsomely housed. Life in these establishments was jolly, and to go to the Hôtel des Haricots was considered a walk in the park, not a punishment.

When the National Guard was abolished, the Hôtel des Haricots found itself without a purpose, and the city turned it into a warehouse for street lighting. In its current form, it makes for a rather curious museum capable of shedding light – no way around that one – on how the streets of Paris have been illuminated in the dark.

There are very few old lanterns left. Those were all sold off to the suburban municipalities, but on the other hand, what a shadeless forest of cast-iron trunks, lyres, and gas and electric lampposts!

You won't see much bronze; the only lampposts made of this expensive alloy are at the opera. In the old days, cast iron was copper-plated, and this copper plating cost nearly 200 francs per lamp.

Nowadays the city is more economical. They simply paint the streetlamps a bronze colour, which costs them about 3 francs.

The tallest and biggest streetlamps are known as the Boulevard Model. Here you can also find the brackets used at corners and in streets with narrow sidewalks.

But still, you might mourn the fact that the city warehouse has sold off so much, and not held onto at least one specimen of each source of light.

There are a few at the Musée Carnavalet, but too few, and photographs of certain models can still be found at the Lepelletier library in Saint-Fargeau.

A visit to the light museum in summertime is not recommended. There's less shade in this grove of metal than in an Australian forest.

But there is shade in the little square.

It was here, on a bench near the gate, that Alexandre Treutens, back from his peregrinations, used to elaborate his lines.

This poet of the people was the poorest of the poor. He composed vaguely humanitarian verses, which he recited to workmen or boatmen in bistros. What obscure reasons led this sad little man to abandon his trade as a shoemaker for poetry? He wandered all over Paris, and whenever he stopped somewhere new – so anxious was he to show his respect for authority – he would subordinate his inspiration to the goodwill of the local mayor. I have seen, with my own eyes, an authentic document issued by the town hall of Enghien, giving a man by the name of Alexandre Treutens permission to practice, 'for the length of one day', in the commune of Enghien, 'the profession of itinerant poet'.

On the left side of rue La Fontaine is a long, dark-grey wall. A door, not easy to get through, leads into a courtyard where some chickens stroll gravely about. To the left, as you enter, you see a pile of strange objects, which I believe are the hoops of old crinolines.

The courtyard is cluttered with bronze and marble statuary of every shape and size.

Apparently one of the statues was sculpted by Rosso. The big bronze deer from the salon of 1911 were lugged in and now stand beside *The Lion's Fiancée*, a bizarre work inspired by a passage in Chamisso:

> Decked with myrtle leaf and roses, the keeper's daughter, before following far away and against her own heart the husband who has come to claim her, goes to say goodbye to her regal childhood friend and give him one last kiss. Mad with grief, the lion dispatches her into dust, then lies down upon the corpse, awaiting the bullet that will strike his heart.

The building on the right is a more or less un-known museum in which one can see a huge canvas by Philippe de Champaigne, a Le Nain called *Saint Jacques* that would be at home in the Louvre, and many paintings.

A few rooms are full of Christs removed from the Palais de Justice.

Élie Delaunay's Christ in particular deserves to be exhibited at the Petit Palais. But it's the profusion of these Christs that is somehow touching. It's like a conference of the crucified. They are all suffering through their administrative exile together.

It occurs to me that, instead of abandoning them like this, it would be better to give them away to poor churches.

This museum is part of the big, mysterious city composed of the old Hôtel des Haricots, behind which stands the forest of lampposts. Here also is the Hall of Prints of the City of Paris and, a short distance away, on an immense plain, the pyramids of cobblestones. These pyramids are constantly in the process of being unmade and remade, and some-times one of them collapses, making a sound like pebbles as the wave recedes.

Separated from this aedile city by rue de Boulain-villiers, a gasworks, with its gas holders, its various buildings, its mountains of coal, its slag heaps and pipsqueak vegetable patches, occupies a lot that stretches to rue du Ranelagh – one of the most deserted zones in the universe. Here you find the home of Monsieur Pierre Mac Orlan, that bright-and-bushy-tailed writer whose imagination brims with cowboys and Foreign Legion soldiers. Seen from the outside, the house in which he lives is un-remarkable. But once you're in, you discover a maze of corridors, staircases, courtyards, and balconies that can be navigated only with difficulty. Mac Orlan's door stands at the end of the darkest corri-dor in the building. His apartment is furnished with rich simplicity. Many books, but well chosen. A Bri-tish policeman in padded wool who changes posture and position according to the whims of the master of the house. Over the fireplace in the main room is a tiny caricature of me by Picasso. Big windows look out onto a wall about three metres away, and if you lean out of one of these a little, you can see the gas holders of all different heights to the left, and, to the right, the railway. At night, the six giant chimneys of the gasworks blaze stupendously:

moon-coloured or blood-coloured, green flames or blue flames. O Pierre Mac Orlan, Baudelaire would have loved the strange mineral landscape you have discovered in Auteuil – the garden district!

If Monsieur Ricciotto Canudo had not moved from Auteuil and founded *Montjoie!* in central Paris, a local legend would have formed about the room he kept in the house at the corner of rue Raynouard and rue Boulainvilliers. I never saw this room myself, but many Auteuil residents had a chance to look in, and for a while it was the talk of the neighbourhood cafés, the busses, and the metro. What surprised the locals was that Monsieur Canudo, who had taken up residence in this hotel, had turned down a furnished room. In fact, it seems, he was on his own furniture, which is to say: a little bed, a table, a chair, and a shelf with some books. The bed, it was said, was very narrow, and I heard one Auteuil resident say, about a thin woman: 'She's as skinny as Monsieur Canudo's bed.'

It was also said that the curtains of the room were always drawn, and that a huge number of candles burned day and night. As a result, Monsieur Canudo was assumed to be the high priest of a new religion whose rites he was performing in his chamber. A few ivy leaves scattered about gave rise to strange suppositions. The one considered most plausible was that Monsieur Canudo was using ivy for purposes of magic, the objective of which had not yet been guessed.

And so it was that the good people of Auteuil voyaged pleasantly and curiously around Monsieur Canudo's room.

But let's walk down to the Seine. It's a lovely river. One never gets tired of looking at it. I have sung about it often, in its diurnal and nocturnal aspects. After the Pont Mirabeau, the promenade attracts no one but poets, locals, and workers in their Sunday best.

Not many Parisians know about the new Quai d'Auteuil. In 1909, it didn't yet exist. The quaisides with their sleazy dives beloved by Jean Lorrain have disappeared. Le Grand Neptune, le Petit Neptune, all those open-air waterfront cafés – what has become of you? The quai has risen to the height of the first floor. The ground floors are earthed up, and the people go in through the windows.

But the most melancholy spot in Auteuil is between Port-Louis and Avenue de Versailles. Théophile Gautier lived at the Boulainvilliers traffic circle, but probably there was not so much scrap metal then as there is today, and Port-Louis did not yet exist, with its brightly coloured fleet of bilanders. On the bridge, there are pots of geraniums and fuchsias; in the planters, there are green trees that grow around a child's little coffin. And when the sun shines, the little coffin of the bilanders isn't gloomy at all.

Monsieur Lehec's Bookshop

Monsieur Lehec the bookseller loved his books so much that he could bring himself to sell them only to the few he deemed worthy of acquiring them.

In the days when he had his bookshop on rue Saint-André-des-Arts, I often used to go in and chat. He was once Victorien Sardou and Anatole France's bookseller, but now, having sold off his stock of good books and gone nearly blind, he keeps his own counsel. Today no one can appeal to his gentle erudition.

One day, as a group of students were walking down rue Saint-André-des-Arts singing the song of Father Dupanloup, which is bawdy enough that it cannot be quoted here, Monsieur Lehec spoke to me of the relationship between the great prelate who well and truly exemplified Dupanloup and two of the most exemplary publishers of satirical and bawdy works, the scholars Isidore Liseux and Alcide Bonneau.

I am not sure whether the famous song of Father Dupanloup has ever been printed, but almost everyone knows it. The song inspired Jules Marry (not the popular novelist) to assemble an excellent anthology called *The Exploits of Monsieur Dupanloup*, a slim volume of verses already becoming rare or destined to become rare soon. As Marry says in the foreword:

> This French song, which is sometimes derisive and sometimes bawdy, spares neither warriors nor churchmen and has transformed its titular prelate into a kind of Christian Priapus or Karagöz. By lending him the most improbable genetic virtues, it has made him a legend in his time. Probably the first rumblings of the song of Father Dupanloup date back to the last years of Louis Philippe's reign.
>
> Monsieur Dupanloup (from *pavone lupus*), whom we encounter in a balloon, on a train, at the Institute and the opera, and, with a bit of artless anachronism, at the crossing of the Berezina, has been the subject of genuine erotic and patriotic worship on the part of our troops,

who, for half a century, have never stopped singing his exploits to get through long marches and
gruelling manoeuvres.

What an odd thing to happen to Monseigneur
Dupanloup's pedagogical preoccupations!

But this prelate, who was, in any event, a holy
man, must have had a sinful power of which history
perhaps furnishes no further examples. For among
his pupils at the minor seminary were Isidore Liseux
and Alcide Bonneau, whose energy and erudition
were most frequently employed in the literary field,
which their teacher's peculiar reputation was to expand in a most unforeseeable manner.

Monsieur Lehec had known Liseux and Bonneau
personally. I recorded his remarks because they
concerned men about whom next to nothing seems
to have been written and who deserve a moment's
attention.

Liseux's publications are more sought after than
ever for their rigour, their beauty, and their rarity.
His chief collaborator was Bonneau, whom he had
befriended at the minor seminary. Both of these
students of Bishop Dupanloup were modesty incarnate. Their styles, marked by extreme precision, are
very similar. Liseux was close-lipped, though I was

told that, when he did open his mouth, it was full of the most biting wit.

During the heyday of Boulangism a man came to Liseux wanting to buy, on the famous general's behalf, a book about oriental ethnology that had not yet been published. Liseux made his apologies and asked where he could send the book when it appeared. He was given the general's address, with this written after Boulanger's name: 'The first of his name of whom anyone has spoken – as was true of Bonaparte.' To which Liseux replied sharply: 'I beg your pardon, but a Bonaparte was present at the siege of Rome in 1527.'

One day, on the quais, he saw a very rare book he could have used but for more than he had on him. So off he went to pawn his watch. But by the time he got back, the book had been sold. Liseux went away in despair. He used to tell this story, always adding: 'I never did redeem the watch. It was a bad onion, which brought forth no tulip.'

Another day he went into an antiques shop for a folio. But the price was too high, and he haggled for so long that the antiques dealer said: 'You drive a hard bargain, but I'm not out to fleece my customers. I keep my prices as low as I can. If my customers aren't happy, I'm not happy. I'm not a bad devil!'

'In that case', said Liseux, 'I'll sell you my soul for your book.'

But in the end he paid for the volume in legal tender.

His printer Motteroz once sued him for being behind on his bills. 'Motteroz is red with anger', said Liseux. 'But megalomania is what it is. He wants us to believe he's Richelieu reincarnate.'

An author submitted a manuscript which he rejected. 'Would the Estiennes or the Elzeviers have printed your book?' asked Liseux. 'No! Do you disagree?... I bid you good day, sir.'

A lady came to offer him a book she had written about Holland: 'The first thing to come to mind is that this would be a book about *Les Pays Bas Bleus*',* Liseux said with a smile. 'You might not think so, madame, but your book would look like a hoax.'

Asked his political views, he replied: 'I am a republican, but of the republic of letters.'

Two bibliophiles were hanging around his shop as he was translating something from English, and

---

* *Les Pays Bas* (the Netherlands); *Les Bas bleus* (Bluestockings).

their chatter began to get on his nerves. The conversation turned to the war of 1770 and Bazaine the traitor. 'Gentlemen', Liseux said, 'one does not speak of rope in the house of a hanged man, nor of traitors in that of a translator.' And all in a dither they hurried out.

Another bibliophile asked for a discount on the books Liseux published, saying he was a friend. 'In that case', the publisher replied, 'you can simply take the books. Don't you know what I have printed on the covers? *For Isidore Liseux and his friends.*' And the bibliophile took the books without paying a cent.

He spoke tenderly of scholarship, as if it were a person and a personal friend. 'She is neither severe', he said, 'nor repulsive. Just think: her body is nature, her head is intelligence, and her finery is books. Bonneau knows her even more intimately than I do. He could tell you what colour her eyes are, and the shade of her hair. He never leaves her side, whereas I have to neglect her sometimes to attend to business.'

When he wanted to publish a translation of some short stories by the Neapolitan storyteller Basile, he was told to talk to a scholar with an exceedingly Germanic name who insisted on signing his translation. 'I would prefer the name *Pulcinella*', Liseux replied, 'or at the very least *Polichinelle*.' And he abandoned his plans.

When his shop was in the Passage Choiseul, Liseux had a clerk and a maid who were brother and sister. The sister's boyfriend became an assistant at the Bibliothèque nationale, in the department where most of Liseux's books are housed. 'I always had the impression', he told me, 'that I was playing second fiddle and she was sleeping with her boss... Her brother, who was my best friend, was watched like a hawk by Monsieur Liseux, who didn't want him coming home to bed later than ten o'clock...''

All in all, Liseux seems to have been a kind and indulgent man. A bad accountant, he was deeply in debt, and his editions cost him a fortune. He was in arrears to his printer and his paper supplier. His funds were dispersed in a manner very disadvantageous to him, and this man, who had published some of the finest books of his day, died in poverty.

In the catalogue of the estate sale, which took place in March 1894, Monsieur Octave Uzanne writes: 'While Jouaust died enchanted and well fed – and rightly condemned by the connoisseurs wronged by the extravagant prices of his productions – Liseux, the dear honest man, died of cold, or who knows what? Perhaps of disgust and weariness, with all of nineteen sous in his pocket!'

Apparently Liseux's papers ended up in the hands of a Belgian bookseller called Van Combrugghe.

None of the details I have scraped together about the life of Bonneau are interesting enough to mention here. He was one of the most discreet and erudite contributors to the Librairie Larousse and led a humble, secluded life. There are still a few people who remember seeing him at the Bibliothèque nationale, where he went often and was not spared aggravation.

I do not know whether he invented it, but he was one of the first to employ the system of literal, line-by-line translations of verse which went on to influence French poetry so profoundly.

In Monsieur Lehec's bookshop, I bought Monsieur Jal's *Virgilius Nauticus*. He had several copies.

It was a pleasure to discover some of Monsier Anatole France's sources of inspiration.

Yet the scholar's name – and Monsieur Jal is not a nonentity – never gets mentioned. Littré always cites him in connection with maritime terms. He is, however, the author of the *Virgilius nauticus* that Anatole France attributes to his Monsieur Bergeret.*

Virgilius Nauticus: An examination of the passages of the Aeneid relating to the navy, by M. Jal, historiographer of the navy and author of works on maritime archaeology... (Paris, Imprimerie Royale, MDCCCXLIII). Such is the title of the book that was to light up the imagination of the most erudite of our contemporary novelists. It is an octavo of 107 pages.

Monsieur Jal, who nods admiringly at Virgil's vast nautical knowledge, was, at least in maritime matters, the sworn enemy of Rabelais and devotes several pages of his *Maritime Archaeology* to Pantagruel's navigations.

'In these pages', he says, 'I analyse the fourth book of the priest of Meudon's immortal work and demonstrate that the learned man knew everything, perhaps, except what concerned seafaring; that he was almost completely ignorant of ships, navigation, and even the vocabulary of mariners; and that if occasionally he stumbled on correct terms in use on ships in the 16th century, it was certainly by

---

* Monsieur Bergeret is a recurring character in Anatole France's series of novels *L'histoire contemporaine*.

accident.'

When he examines the technical side of naval life in the *Aeneid*, Jal comes to the opposite conclusion.

After describing the very young Virgil studying mathematics in Naples and Milan, he writes of the eighteen years the poet spent in Naples, Sicily, Campania.

> All through these years, he would have constantly been seeing the military fleet stationed in the port of Misenum, and the rich convoys bearing the treasures of Greece and Egypt to Panormus, Messana, Megara Hyblaea, Syracuse, and Parthenope, and the pleasure-boats owned by the wealthy voluptuaries whose elegant houses, constructed around the Crater, were reflected in the calm waters of that magnificent bay.

Later Jal lingers on this bay:

> It was criss-crossed by a thousand boats, each vying to go faster than the rest and all proudly on parade, with their silver or golden prows, their sterns surmounted by flamboyantly curved aphlastons, and their graceful chenisci over tutelary figures. Some of their oars were covered with mother-of-pearl or bands of precious metal;

most of their rigging was made of many-coloured wool; and almost all of their sails were woven from purple or the finest white linen, decorated with erotic images and some maxim or other, inscribed next to the owner's name, borrowed from a sensual philosophy.

Jal is merciless with annotators and translators of Virgil who fail to recognize the poet's erudite exactitude. Badius Ascensius is unequipped for the ingenious explanation of the word *puppes*; 'Father de La Rue is at a loss as to why prows and sterns are opposites'; Annibale Caro substitutes vessels for prows; Gregorio Hernández de Velasco treats Virgil very cavalierly; João Franco Barreto is more scrupulous, but not much more; Dryden mistakes the prows and sterns for the ships themselves; John Voss's German translation leaves as much to be desired as Dryden's English version; and Delille, the most esteemed of the French translators, has, like his foreign rivals, not intimately understood his author's text.

As for Virgil's nautical terms, the learned Jal goes so far as to cite words from the language of the Malays, the Malagasy, and the New Zealanders. He makes even more picturesque connections when he examines the phrase *triplici versu*:

It expresses, in my opinion, a chant repeated three times, a cry, a hurrah, a kind of *celeusma* whose tradition is still alive and well on ships where, when there's heavy work to be done – for example, when the bowlines are being hauled in, a sailor, the true *hortator* of the old ships, sings: *One, two, three! Hurrah!* The ancient tradition was still strong in medieval Venice, where the galley master of the bucentaur, whenever the ducal ship passed the monastery of the Virgin at the entrance to the Arsenal, used to shout three times, 'Ah! Ah! Ah!', pounding the oars after each acclamation.

Jal's conclusion is no doubt different from the one our contemporary Monsieur Bergeret would have found for his famous work:

The navy of today is very similar to the navy of the past; this, to me, could not be clearer. And this is why I think that any man who occupies himself with modern naval life must inquire into every particular of the ancient navies. It is also why I think – given that Virgil is, with regard to the ancient navy, the writer who can be most pro-ductively consulted – it was necessary to demonstrate and furnish proof of competence, restoring to his verses all of their didactic value, which was been stripped away by interpreters who may have been very learned but who did not understand the special language spoken by the sea poet.

Monsieur Anatole France may well have purchased a copy of *Virgilius Nauticus* from Monsieur Lehec, in whose shop he sometimes used to linger for an hour. One day, I happened to hear him praising Abbé Delille.

'Delille's only failing', said Monsieur Anatole France, 'is that he is not read.'

And having memorized long declamations, he recited them.

I suspect he has not retained quite so many lines written by his master, Leconte de Lisle.

But isn't there a certain kinship between the two poets?

After hearing someone compare Leconte de Lisle and Abbé Delille, I remembered having read, in an article, an opinion that struck me as at the very least unusual. I have just found it expressed again and again in two different pieces penned by Louis Veuillot:

All this faded descriptive finery – all this clangour of colour and light – what are they but old Abbé Delille's hand-me-downs? Under this cargo of circumlocutions, only Jacques Delille has walked with a nimble step. The lapdog of the salons, whose pretty little paws pattered unflinching through the porcelain, occasionally upsetting some pretty fake pearls, has by now become an elephant burdened with a battle tower full of fierce – and above all colourful – soldiers. Leconte de Lisle simulates the loaded march well. But the earth fails to tremble.

A few days later, Veuillot added:

De Lisle describes to excess. We have recalled the other Delille, his near namesake, who may seem to be his opposite. But in truth, there is not much difference between them. The two extremes touch. Both men make a priority of description because they lack the gift of imagination, the gift of feeling, and perhaps the gift of thinking. They have only the external eye – the outer skin of poetry; the sap and the source are unknown to them. The old Delille, who made do with being a philosopher and pretending at correctness, would nowadays be an irregular and perhaps pedantic freethinker. He would write Kain with a K and think nothing of *Kainite* and *Khaldean*. The young de Lisle – fifteen lustra back – would have gone in for *gardens*, *imagination*, *reading*, *coffee*, and *chess*, and been a past master at painting Iris and the rocks in soft blues. They are the same man, ignorant of humanity, practicing the same childish game at the same level of skill. Only one was born under the sign of Voltaire and the other under Victor Hugo.

If there is a difference to be noted, perhaps the imagination of the old Delille was not quite so limited as the new one. As far as we can judge, from the distance we now have from his works and his time, Abbé Jacques drew less from the public funds. Monsieur Leconte de Lisle's descriptions are stuffed to the gills with the physical prompts provided by architecture, statuary, painting, and drawing, from which all our materialist poetry borrows considerably, above all in the vast and abundant domains of their vagaries.

I am in any case inclined to think that Abbé Delille's art exerted a real influence on the Parnassians.

They did not claim to be his followers because by then he was a much-maligned poet, and probably, at the Parnassus Choiseul,* it was de rigueur to speak of Leconte de Lisle and not of Jacques Delille.

Monsieur Anatole France was making restitution on rue Saint-André-des-Arts.

The bookshop still exists, its appearance unchanged, and is now run by another bookseller who knows his trade, though he does not have Monsieur Lehec's superstitious respect for books.

---

* Phrase used by Louis Veuillot to mock *Le Parnasse contemporain*, published by Alphonse Lemerre, whose shop was in the Passage Choiseul.

1, Rue Bourbon-le-Château

On 23 December 1850, two women were murdered in this old building. One of them was Mademoiselle Ribault, a cartoonist for the *Petit Courrier des Dames* edited by Monsieur Thiéry. As she was dying, she found the strength to dip her finger in her own blood and write on a folding screen: 'The murder was committed by Mr. Thi's clerk.' Laforcade, the clerk in question, was arrested a few hours later for his crime.

Today the building attracts the attention of the curious for another reason.

It is home to Monsieur André Mary, the Burgundian poet to whom Monsieur Fernard Fleuret dedicated his satiric macaronic *Falourdin*, stigmatising the contemporary press.

Early in this poem, Fleuret sings of the old house on rue Bourbon-le-Château:

> If you translate, let's say, a mouldy Boethius
> In your gloomy house at Carrefour Buci
> Where the books are copious and all the pots
> Chinese...

The author of *Falourdin* – who can be reproached for no more than a little archaism, if indeed such a rare fault merits reproach – is today, at a time when they are rare, one of the best writers of French verse, and being truly a poet, his productions deserve to be passed down to ages to come...

Monsieur Fleuret is a Norman. Once, during a banquet celebrating the thousandth anniversary of Normandy, a giant Norwegian standing next to him looked down his nose and declared: 'You, little Viking; me, big Viking.' The little Viking, to quote another Norman poet, looks like an archer out of the Bayeux Tapestry.

One day, when he was still a schoolboy, his strong proclivity for pranks led him to convince his parents' cook that a certain sheathe, which had been named long ago after the peaceable city of Condom, was a new style of purse perfect for large coins. An outburst of laughter at the butcher's soon spread through the town. The cook complained bitterly, making no secret of her deceiver's name. And from that day forward, the devout looked askance at Monsieur Fernand Fleuret.

When he was seeking to publish a literary hoax far superior to Mérimée's, titled *The Quiver of Sieur Louvigné du Dézert*, Fleuret sought the support of a publisher who lives near the Odéon.

The publisher smiled at my Fleuret, fondled the manuscript, and opened it. The first word his eye fell upon is one the typographers bungled so badly that later, in a newspaper, there would be talk of the digs of Madame Dieulafoy.

'*Digs*, monsieur!' cried the publisher, closing the manuscript. 'Monsieur... I must ask you to leave my office.'*

Monsieur Maurice Cremnitz still lives in the 'gloomy house at Carrefour Buci'. He once aroused a good deal of curiosity by publishing, under the initials MC, in *Vers et Prose*, an excellent poem in memory of Jean Moréas titled 'Anniversaire'.

---

* Untranslatable pun. The word for digs is *fouilles*, but Apollinaire would seem to be hinting at the word *foutre* (more or less equivalent to *fuck*), as in, in the poem in question: 'Ha ! ha ! foutre des Dieux.' (Ha! Ha! Fuck the Gods!)

Monsieur Cremnitz has not shown his work for many years now. His friends, the poets, put great stock in the integrity of his taste, and if his decisions are not decrees, they do generally win the approval of the person who has prompted them, and who abides by them. The authority he exercises, with great discretion and in a very small circle, gives him an unexpected role in contemporary literature. It was not a role he sought and comes with many responsibilities.

Every year during peacetime, Cremnitz, a committed rambler, would go walking through a region he hadn't yet seen much of. He didn't bother with luggage. With a good cane in hand, he walked and walked, stopping as he pleased, never giving a thought to timetables.

Once, near Montereau, two policemen stopped him on the road and asked for his papers.

Patting himself down, Cremnitz found only an entry card to the Bibliothèque nationale. The policeman examined it, and one of them said: 'So this is where you work?' When Cremnitz said yes, he replied: 'Your employer must not pay very well if you can't even take the train.'

Monsieur Cremnitz is not well known to the new generations, though André Gide and Léon-Paul Fargue have not forgotten him. He enlisted as soon as the war broke out.

When I saw him again in Nice, he was in his in-fantry uniform.

He was living the life of the regimental depots then. We would see each other in cafés for a few minutes, and as an infantryman, he thought that I, an artilleryman, was better dressed. I was almost ashamed of this, and when I said goodbye, I would walk away backwards to avoid upsetting this kind and valiant young man with the glare of my spurs.

I met a few other literary soldiers in Nice and Nîmes during my military training. For example the playwright Auguste Achaume, a corporal in a terri-torial regiment. He cut a fine figure in his greatcoat and, stationed in a skating rink, used to sleep on the orchestra platform; at present, he sleeps in a tent. In the artillery depot where I was finishing my 'courses', my bed was next to that of a poet corporal, René Berthier, a member of the Facettes literary group in Toulon. I have read some of his poems, and in my opinion he is one of the best of his genera-tion. He is now a second lieutenant in the artillery.

In addition to being a poet, he is a first-rate savant, responsible for innumerable inventions useful to humanity.

In Nîmes, I also saw Léo Larguier again. He had visited the house at 1, rue Bourbon-le-Château many times, and published a beautiful literary book about the war called *Les Heures perdues*.

On the first Sunday in March 1915, I was having lunch at the little restaurant de la Grille, when a corporal of the line stood up from a table and came over, reciting some lines from 'The Song of the Badly Loved'.

I was speechless. A second gunner and driver is not accustomed to having his own poems recited to his face. I looked at but did not recognize him. He was tall and reminded me of a beardless Victor Hugo or, even more, a clean-shaven Balzac. Then he spoke: 'I am Léo Larguier. How are you, Guillaume Apollinaire?' And we were together till evening, when it was time to head back to barracks. On that day and the days that followed, we didn't talk about the war, because soldiers never talk about it, but about the flora of Nîmes, in which, whatever Moréas says, jasmine doesn't figure. Monsieur Bertin, the secretary general of the prefecture, used to join us, giving us the pleasure of his conversation and witty erudition. The direful voice of Léo Larguier dominated these colloquies, and even now I can hear the detonations whenever he uttered name of a man in his company: Ferragute Cypriaque.

One Sunday Larguier took me and Monsieur Bertin to visit a friend of his, the painter Sainturier, whose drawings are as pure as Despiau's. Sainturier lives like a hermit, is unknown, and revels in his sunny Southern obscurity. Though past the age of service, he looks quite young, is robust, works constantly, and in addition to his productions, which are not for sale, his house contains artistic treasures of a kind I never would have suspected.

It was in Sainturier's house that I saw an extraordinary portrait of Stendhal, half-length and straight on. His face is calm and sparkles with suppressed malice. It was also there that I saw Alfred de Musset for the first time. All the other portraits of him look artificial once you clap eyes on this one by Ricard. Musset is in profile. Larguier could hardly believe it, and Sainturier promised to make him a copy after the war. He also had a beautiful portrait of Manet by Ricard. Besides this, we saw a Van Dyck (*Charles I as a Child*), several portraits and miniatures by Isabey, an El Greco, some sketches by Boucher, a marvellous Latour, two Hubert Roberts, some Monticellis, a small still life by Cézanne, and on and on.

I didn't see Larguier again the next day. He had already left for a training camp, and from there he went to the front as a corporal in the stretcher-bearers. We were not far from each other at the Battle of Champagne, but meeting up was out of the question. He was wounded in that battle, and we did not see each other again until he was on leave, right there, precisely in front of No. 1, Rue Bourbon-le-Château – that 'gloomy house' sung by Fernand Fleuret.

Christmas Carols on rue Buci

You should have gone and seen rue de Buci – so precious to the poets of my generation – on the night of 24 December before the war. In a garden flat on rue Buci, André Salmon, Maurice Cremnitz, René Dalize and I once had a Christmas Eve feast. We listened to carols whose words I jotted down in shorthand. They were from all different regions of France.

Carols must be one of the most curious monuments of French religious and popular poetic traditions. In any event they are the creations that perhaps best reflect the soul and customs of the provinces they come from. The first one I recorded in the cellar on rue de Buci was belted out by a barber's assistant born in Bourg-en-Bresse.

Clearly Christmases in Bresse are nothing like our wartime Christmases.

The Rabelaisian enumeration of victuals could not be a farther cry from the restrictions of the deprived era in which we live.

Dès que la ville de Bourg – En apprit la nouvelle, – On fit battre le tambour – Pour mettre tout par écuelles. – Les bécasses, les levrauts – Les cailles, les chapons gras – Furent pris chez Curnillon – Pour faire la bourdifaille – Furent pris chez Gurnillon – Pour faire le réveillon.

Gog porta trois dindonneaux – Et farcit une belle oie, – Et d'une longe de veau – Il fit un bon ragoût ; – Sa femme fit du boudin – Et prit chez monsieur de Choin – Une grande bassine d'argent, – Pour y, pour y, pour y mettre – Une grande bassine d'argent — Pour y mettre son présent.

On alla vite appeler – L'hôte de la Bonne École – Qui porta des godiveaux – Et prit une belle andouille ; – Il mêla des fricandeaux – Avec des oreilles de veaux – Et porta trois barillets – De mou, de mou, de moutarde, – Et porta trois barillets – De moutarde de Dijon.

Quand l'hôte de Saint-François – Entendit qu'on faisait bruire – Les poêles et les lèchefrites – Dans le quartier de Tesnière, – Il fit faire à son valet – Une potringue de poulet – Qu'on s'en léchait tout droit – Les ba, les ba, les babines – Qu'on s'en léchait tout droit – Les babines et les cinq doigts.

Dès que l'hôte de l'Écu – Vit qu'on partait au clair de lune, – Il mit pour quatre écus – De sucre dans la farine – Pour lui faire des gâteaux – Qui semblèrent des châteaux ; – ils sont meilleurs que le pain – Pour les, pour les, pour les dames ; – Ils sont meilleurs que le pain – Pour les dames et les enfants.

Neren mit dessus une planche – Du boudin blanc comme neige – Et douze langues de bœuf – Qui étaient noires comme pain ; – Et puis de son bon vin vieux – Que j'ai souvent bu, – Et boirai, s'il plaît à Dieu. – Jusqu'à, jusqu'à, jusqu'à Pâques, – Et boirai, s'il plaît à Dieu, – Plus qu'il ne veut m'en donner.

À nous deux, père Alexis, – Il nous faut faire une offrande – Et nous joindre cinq ou six – Pour toucher une sarabande ; – Avec notre gros bourdon – Nous chanterons tout de bon ; – Noël, Noël est venu – Nous ferons la bourdifaille – Noël, Noël est venu, – Nous ferons du brouet moulu.*

---

* This 'religioso-culinary' carol from Bresse is recorded in *Chansons populaires des provinces de France* (1860). Truly a Rabelaisian celebration of Christmastime feasting, it begins: 'When the town of Bourg / Heard the news, / They beat the tambour / And ladled out the food', which includes woodcocks, leverets, quails, capons, turkeys, a goose, veal, andouille, fricandeaux, calves' ears, ox tongues, black and white puddings, and (for the 'la-la-la ladies') cakes as big as castles. All

To follow this carol, here is a more graceful one I heard again a few years back near Saint-Quentin. I give the version I recorded on rue de Buci:

Chantons, je vous prie, – Noël hautement – D'une voix jolie – En solennisant – De Marie pucelle – La Conception – Sans originelle – Maculation.

Cette jeune fille – Native elle était – De la noble ville – Dite Nazareth, – de vertu remplie – De corps gracieux – C'est la plus jolie – Qui soit sous les cieux.

Elle allait au Temple ; – Pour Dieu supplier ; – Le conseil s'assemble – Pour la marier ; – La fille tant belle – N'y veut consentir, – Car Vierge et pucelle – Veut vivre et mourir.

L'Ange leur commande – Qu'on fasse assembler – Gens en une bande, – Tous à marier ; – Et duquel la verge – Tantôt fleurira – À la noble Vierge – Vrai mari fera.

Tantôt abondance – De gentils galants – La vierge plaisante – S'en vont souhaitant ; – À la noble fille –

---

the landowners chip in, and by the end of the song, the wine is flowing: 'O Father Alexis, you and I / Must make an offering / Then tie on five or six / Till the night's fiddlesticks / And we really start to sing / Christmas is here, Christmas is here / Let's drink in good cheer / Christmas is here, Christmas is here / Egg custard for you and me.'

Chacun s'attendait, – Mais le plus habile – Sa peine y perdait.

Joseph prit sa verge, – Pour s'y en venir : – Combien qu'à la Vierge – N'eût mis son désir ; – Car toute la vie – N'eut intention – Vouloir ni envie – De conjonction.

Quand furent au Temple – Trétous assemblés, – Étant tous ensemble – En troupe ordonnés, – La verge plaisante – De Joseph fleurit, – Et au même instant – Porta fleur et fruit.

En grande révérence – Joseph on retint, – Qui par sa main blanche – Cette vierge print ; – Puis après le prêtre, – Recteur de la loi, – Leur a fait promettre – À tous deux la foi.

Baissant les oreilles – Ces gentils galants – Tant que c'est merveille, – S'en vont murmurant – Disant c'est dommage – Que ce père gris – Ait en mariage – Cette vierge pris.

La nuit ensuivante, – Autour de minuit, – La Vierge plaisante – En son livre lit, – Que le Roi céleste – Prendrait nation – D'une pucelette – Sans corruption.

Tandis que Marie – Ainsi contemplait – Et du tout ravie – Envers Dieu était, – Gabriel archange – Vint subitement – Entrant dans sa chambre – Tout visiblement.

D'une voix doucette – Gracieusement – Dit à la fillette – En la saluant : – Dieu vous gard, Marie, –

Pleine de beauté, – Vous êtes l'Amie – Du Dieu de bonté.

Dieu fait un mystère – En vous merveilleux, – C'est que serez mère – Du roi glorieux ; – Votre pucelage – Et virginité – Par divin ouvrage – Vous sera gardé.

À cette parole – La Vierge consent, – Le Fils de Dieu vole, – En elle descend. – Bientôt fut enceinte – Du prince des Rois, – Sans mal ni complainte – Le porta neuf mois.

La noble besogne – Joseph pas n'entend. – À peu qu'il n'en grogne, – S'en va murmurant ; – Mais l'ange céleste – Lui dit, en dormant, – Qu'il ne s'en déhaite, – Par Dieu est l'enfant.

Joseph et Marie – Tous deux Vierges sont, – Qui par compagnie – En Bethléem vont. – Là est accouchée – En pauvre déduit – La Vierge sacrée – Autour de minuit.

Y fut consolée – des anges des cieux, Y fut visitée – Des Pasteurs joyeux, – Y fut révérée – De trois nobles Rois, – Et fut rejetée – Des nobles bourgeois.

Or, prions Marie – Et Jésus, son fils, – Qu'après cette vie – Ayons Paradis – Et, notre voyage – Étant achevé, – Nous donne en partage – Le ciel azuré. *

---

* A Marian carol celebrating the virgin birth of Jesus, the lyrics mix sacred language with the tropes of secular ballads: Mary, the most beautiful girl in the Nazareth, wishes to remain a maiden but is fated to be wed to the good Joseph, is visited by the archangel Gabriel, and carries Jesus in her womb for nine months 'without pain or complaint'.

This charming carol is still sung in May-en-Multien. Here is a verse:

Bergers qu'on s'assemble – Au signal donné – Pour aller ensemble – Saluer tourelourirette – Saluer louladerirette – Le roi nouveau né. *

This one too is still sung:

Saint Liphard alla prendre – La Dame du Chemin – À dessein de s'y rendre – tenant tous en leurs mains – Hautbois, Luths et Guitares – Pour faire des fanfares, – Trompettes et tambours – Pour jouer tout le jour. †

Here is another carol I heard on rue de Buci. I don't know where it comes from. It's very rustic and full of panache:

Refrain : *Laissez paître vos bêtes, – Pastoureaux par monts par vaux, – Laissez paître vos bêtes – Et venez chanter Nau.*

---

* 'Shepherds, let us gather / At the prearranged signal / And let us go / To greet the tra-la-la-ling / The la-la-la-ling / The newborn king.'

† 'Saint Liphardus went to fetch / La Dame du Chemin / So as to travel / With all in their hands / Oboes and lutes, / Drums, trumpets, and flutes / To play the fanfaronade / All day long.'

J'ai ouï chanter le rossignol – Qui chantait un chant si nouveau – Si haut, si beau, – Si raisonneau, – Il m'y rompait la tête, – Tant il prêchait et caquetait, – Ai donc pris ma houlette – Pour aller voir Nolet (refrain).

Je m'enquis au berger Nolet ; – As-tu ouï le Rossignolet – Tant joliet – Qui gringottait – Là-haut sur une épine ? – Ah oui ! dit-il, je l'ai ouï, – J'en ai pris ma bucine – Et m'en suis réjoui (refrain).

Nous dîmes tous une chanson, – Les autres sont venus au son. – Or, sus, dansons. – Prends Alizon ! – Je prendrai Guillemette, – Margot prendra le gros Guillot. – Qui prendra Péronnelle ? – Ce sera Talebot (refrain).

Ne dansons plus, nous tardons trop ; – Allons tôt, courons le trot, – Viens-t'en bientôt. – Attends, Guillot, – J'ai rompu ma courette, – Il faut ramender mon sabot. – Or, tiens cette aiguillette, – Elle t'y servira trop (refrain).

Comment, Guillot, ne viens-tu pas ? – Eh oui, j'y vais tout le doux pas, – Tu n'entends pas – Trestout mon cas ; – J'ai aux talons les mules, – C'est pourquoi je ne puis trotter ; – Prises m'ont les froidures. – En allant estraquer (refrain).

Marche devant, pauvre Mulard, – et t'appuye sur ton billart ; – Et toi, Coquard, – Vieux Loriquart, – Tu dois avoir grand honte – De rechigner ainsi les dents,

– Et dois n'en tenir compte – Au moins devant les gens (refrain).

Nous courûmes de telle roideur, – Pour voir Notre doux Rédempteur – Et créateur – Et formateur ; – Il avait, Dieu le sache, – De drapeaux assez grand besoin ; – Il gisait dans la crèche – Sur un petit de foin (refrain).

Sa mère avecque lui était – Un vieillard si lui éclairait – Point ne semblait – Au beau douillet – Il n'était pas son père – Je l'aperçus bien au museau – Ressemblait à la mère – Encor est-il plus beau (refrain).

Or, nous avions un grand paquet – De vivres pour faire un banquet ; – Mais le muguet – De Jean Huguet – Et une grande Levrière – Mirent le pot à découvert ; – Puis ce fut la bergère – Qui laissa l'huis ouvert (refrain).

Pas ne laissâmes de gaudir ; – Je lui donnai une brebis ; – Au petit fils – Une mauvis – Lui donna Péronnelle, – Et Margot lui donna de lait – Une petite écuelle – Couverte d'un volet (refrain).

Or, prions tous le Roi des Rois – Qu'il nous donne à tous bon Noël – Et bonne paix – De nos méfaits, – Ne veuille avoir mémoire – De nos péchés, nous pardonner, – À ceux du Purgatoire – Leurs péchés effacer (refrain).*

---

* A dancing carol in which the shepherd-singer hears the song of a nightingale and asks another shepherd, Nolet, whether he has heard it too. They themselves start to sing,

Here is a delicate and delectable carol. I regret I got down only these few lines:

Je me suis levé par un matinet – Que l'aube prenait son blanc mantelet. – Chantons Nolet, Nolet, Nolet, – Chantons Nolet encore. *

And a jam-packed carol:

Célébrons la naissance – Nostri salvatoris – Qui fait la complaisance – Dei sui patris. – Ce Sauveur tant aimable – In nocte media – Est né dans une étable – De Casta Maria. †

---

and soon others come running: Alizon, Margot, fat Guillot et al. Everyone dances for a spell before going to celebrate Christmas, praying to the King of Kings to forget their misdeeds, forgive their transgressions, and cancel the sins of the souls in Purgatory. The oft-repeated refrain runs: 'Let your animals graze, / Shepherds, over hill and dale, / Let your animals graze / And come sing Noel.'

* 'I woke up one morning / As the dawn shouldered its white cloak. / Let us sing Noel, Noel, Noel, / Let us sing again Noel.'

† Probably Apollinaire calls this carol 'jam-packed' because of all the interlarded Latin. 'Let us celebrate the birth / *Nostri salvatoris* / The clement one / *Dei sui patris.* / This gentle Savior / *In nocte media* / Was born in a stable / *De Casta Maria.*'

On that same Christmas Eve, I also recorded this carol from a province now devastated by the war, the Champagne of La Fontaine and Paul Fort:

Les filles de Cernay – Ne furent endormies. – Avecques beurre et lait – Tout's aux champs se sont mies, – Et celles de Taissy – Ont passé la chaussée – Après avoir oï – Le bruit – Et le riant débat – La, la ! – De celles de Sillery.*

And finally someone sang a graceful children's carol, which must have been of very recent vintage. Here is a verse:

Une petite abeille – Bourdonnant en frelon – s'approcha du poupon, – Lui disant à l'oreille – J'apporte du bonbon ; – Il est doux à merveille ; – Goûtez-en mon mignon.†

---

* This carol from Champagne is also recorded in *Chansons populaires des provinces de France* (1860). 'The girls of Cernay / Were not asleep. / With butter and milk / They all went to the fields, / And those of Taissy / Went over the causeway / When they heard / The noise / And the laughing voices / La, la! Of the girls of Sillery.'

† 'A little bee / Buzzing like a hornet / Flew up to the baby / And said in his ear / I bring you candy; / It's wonderfully sweet; / Taste it, my darling.'

One might take away a hundred different impressions from the old rue de Buci. I would give them all for the feelings I had as I listened to these carols being sung one Christmas Eve, a few years before the war.

From Le Napo to Ernest La Jeunesse's Room

Sometimes I go sit for a moment at the end of the day on the terrace of Le Napo, well reputed for its ice-creams. The Café Napolitain, on the boulevards, was once a very popular literary café. You still see literary and theatre people there. But the great literary era was before the war, when you would always find Jean Moréas, Catulle Mendès, the Silvains, and above all Ernest La Jeunesse, the king of the courtiers...

But I did not meet the author of *The Boulevard* at Le Napo...

One day in 1907, as I was leaving Boulevard des Italians for rue de Grammont, a piece of white paper, leafing along before me, caught my attention.

Instinctively I picked up what I assumed to be a flyer. But just then I looked up at the third floor of a building nearby and saw a masked figure, who immediately drew back, shouting: 'Hold onto that paper, sir, I will come down to retrieve it posthaste.'

I waited for five or six minutes, and when no one came, I went into the building, meaning to give the paper to the concierge, who could then hand it over to the third-floor tenant, but the concierge replied: 'You must be mistaken; there is no one living on the third floor. That apartment is for let. Twelve thousand a month.'

Concealing my surprise, I pretended to be rereading an address on the paper, and claiming I had misread the number, I was just about to leave, proferring my apologies, but just as I went to open the glass door, I saw my mask, in the process of unmasking, scurry by. He appeared, in the little glimpse I had of him, to be a freshly shaven blond man. By this point the whole little series of events struck me as so mysterious that I no longer had any wish to return the stray piece of paper. I was intrigued and, also, in a state of agitation. I turned to the concierge and asked about the apartment in question, saying that as a matter of fact I was looking for a place to let and perhaps, after all, I might relocate to the boulevard. A few moments later, I was touring the empty third-floor rooms with the concierge and saw no evidence at all of the strange goings-on that had piqued my interest. Soon I was out the door again, eager to take a closer look at the piece of paper, which I was sure contained a serious secret.

In the street I saw no sign of the man. I suspected that when he no longer saw me from his third-floor perch he decided I must have headed down rue de Grammont, froze, and was now considering running after me and finally catching up.

I went back the way I'd come, up rue de Richelieu, to the Palais-Royal, where, in a quiet brasserie, I endeavoured to decipher the contents of the troublesome document. I saw, written in an inexpert hand, the following signs: A. B. C. D. E. F. G. H. I. J. K. L. M. N. O. P. Q. S. T. U. V. W. X. Y. Z. Next to these capital letters, a crude drawing depicted a man with two jets of flame on his forehead beside which a 1 sat just above a 5. I was in the presence of a rebus, but I quickly realized it was nothing like those trivial rebuses you still find in certain newspapers, which, at cafés in the evening, parochial Oedipuses sit down and decipher. The rebus in question denoted an ancient art. The person who had composed it was clearly familiar with the popular symbolism behind the rebuses of Picardy, in which medieval pamphleteers painted what they would not have dared to say openly and what the people, not knowing how to read, could understand only in images. Thanks to compulsory education, the writer of my rebus no longer had any reason not to include letters and numbers and therefore had made use of them, adulterating the Picard art with the methods of Renaissance scholars, in which a decadence of the rebus could already be detected. I therefore knew that, in order to decipher this rebus, I need not seek an exact connection between the visible signs and what they meant or how they were pronounced. In a nutshell: I noted that all the letters of the alphabet were written on the paper except *R*, that the man with the two horns of fire on his forehead was Moses, and that the 1 over the 5 amply indicated, given that these numerals were right next to the Hebrew legislator, the first book of the Pentateuch, and the rebus could obviously be read as follows: *R n'est là, genèse*, which undoubtedly signified: Ernest La Jeunesse.*

---

* Untranslatable play on words: *R n'est là, genèse* literally means 'R is not there, Genesis', but is pronounced, if you run the words together, like Ernest la Jeunesse.

Thus this bizarre adventure came to an end, in the name of the author of *Les nuits, les ennuis, et les âmes de nos plus notoires contemporains*; *L'Imitation de notre maître Napoléon*; *Cinq ans chez les sauvages*; and many other works that bubble over with a subtle verve. I resolved to go visit Ernest La Jeunesse at his home, and though we had never met, he kindly welcomed me the very next morning in the building where he lived – a building at the end of a faraway boulevard near the Bastille. And there I am, in the abode of this new author of *Les nuits*, a Musset who is not, like the old one, the poet of youth, but Youth incarnate.*
I scarcely register him, however, and my hello is mechanical. His room has my full attention. The whole floor is chockablock with beautifully bound books; enamelwork; objects made of ivory, rock crystal, and mother-of-pearl; compasses; pottery from Rhodes and Damascus; Chinese bronzes. To the left of the door, on a white wooden table, is a profusion of cameos and intaglios, archaic Greek gems, Etruscan scarabs, rings, seals, African statuettes, games, netsuke, Chelsea Toys, cups, and chalices. In front of the table, against the left-hand wall, running all the way to the

---

* Musset wrote a series of poems entitled *Les Nuits*; La Jeunesse, in French, means 'Youth'.

other end of the room, is an immense mountain of books, weapons of every ancient and modern variety, military equipment, canes, paintings, etc. To the right of the door, the open night table reveals a vase fit to burst with old watches, and beyond that a small iron bed above which the walls are covered all the way to the ceiling with many miniatures of military men. At the foot of the bed is another pile of weapons, as well as rare fabrics, helmets, and wax portraits in their glass boxes.

At the window, on a round table, a collection of ancient bonbons, coloured sugar figurines, tiny confectionary houses, and little fondant sheep arrayed around a big Italian Easter lamb seems to have been prepared more than a century ago for a turbulent flock of kids who never came, who grew up, grew old, and died without having touched these antiquated, alluring pieces of confectionery, precious objects for the gourmandise of yore, whose history has not yet been written and doesn't even have its own museum.

I looked at Ernest La Jeunesse all dressed to go out, a beaver hat on his head and a beautiful reed walking stick in hand, waiting for me to break free from the spell of astonishment cast by his little room.

Ernest La Jeunesse was a solidly built man. I will leave it to others to describe him, his jewellery, and his canes, but I do want to mention his voice, which had a very high timbre. I soon became convinced that his way of speaking, in a high soprano voice, was the result of neither chance nor an accident. It was a hygienic practice, which Ernest La Jeunesse conscientiously followed. Speaking with a head voice purifies the soul, clarifies one's thoughts, even improves one's willpower and decision-making.

I held up the rebus, and for a moment Ernest La Jeunesse looked dumbfounded. But he quickly pulled himself together and told me it was just one of those things he scribbled in a café, but copied by an ignoramus. Then he changed the subject.

It was time for Ernest La Jeunesse to go out. He invited me to go with him, and at Le Napo, where we stopped, someone came over and asked the names of the officers of such and such a cavalry regiment. Monsieur La Jeunesse rattled them off and, seeing my surprise, told me he knew the whole *Military Yearbook* by heart. Then he reminded me that a few years earlier he had, in a discussion of tactics, 'stumped' the minister of war himself in a public forum. And Ernest La Jeunesse drew a portrait of this minister and himself, and then one of Napoleon, and gave them all to me.

He shouted: 'Bring me my child's sabre!'

This was brought, and piece by piece he had the staff show me every item in an arsenal that he owned and kept in storage at the café. At that point, a gentleman, who struck me as a person of quality, with an accent whose national origins eluded me, came over to ask my companion about certain details concerning the genealogy of a ruling family. Ernest La Jeunesse rattled them off without being asked twice, after which he told me he knew the whole *Gotha* by heart...

At that, we parted, and off Ernest La Jeunesse went to inquire about a play he had deposited several years earlier at I don't know which theatre – a play titled, I believe, *La Dynastie*.

I saw him often after that at Le Napolitain, where he passed a large part of his days now that the Bols and the Kalisaya were gone.

He died of throat cancer on 2 May 1917 at the Bon-Secours nursing home on rue des Plantes, aged forty-three.

Born in 1874, this boy from Lorraine, who all through his youth dreamed of conquering Paris, became almost famous overnight among literary and theatre people, art lovers and fencers.

It all started with a very strange coup: the praise of Édouard Drumont, who, not knowing that Ernest La Jeunesse was Jewish, wrote an enthusiastic review of his first book.

This first book did more for its author's reputation than anything he wrote later.

It was the one called *Les Nuits, les ennuis et les âmes de nos plus notoires contemporains*, which came before, and displayed much more discerning imagination and nuanced irony, than the famous *À la manière de...** imitated by the higher-ups in the mess-halls at the rear of the front, who, if these were the old days, would be busy translating Horace into French verse.

Les Nuits et les ennuis amused everyone mentioned in its pages. Reviews abounded, and the author's reputation was made.

---

* A series of books by Paul Reboux and Charles Müller full of imitations of famous authors, including Racine, Chateaubriand, and Mallarmé.

His style of dress did come into it a little. It was dishevelled – not dishevelled à la Verlaine, but dishevelled with an embellishment of amethyst rings, extraordinary canes, sensational charms – in a word, the dishevelment of a boulevardier.

From his first day in Paris, La Jeunesse had stayed in the same room in the building on Boulevard Beaumarchais where I met him. And there he remained until, not long before the war, the profits earned from his anonymous contributions to *Le Petit Café* allowed him to expand his collection of helmets, weapons, Napoleonic cast-offs, books, canes, miniatures, medals, and coins – piled up in that room until they almost reached the ceiling – by transporting them elsewhere. Those who were admitted into the old mare's nest remember the chamber pot spilling over with antique watches.

Sometimes, in the days of *La Revue Blance*, Ernest La Jeunesse used to wander over to rue de l'Échaudé, where sometimes his friend Jarry did his best to drive him round the bend.

Once, in later years, he went with Moréas to the Closerie des Lilas.

As a rule, however, he kept to the right bank, or more precisely to the boulevards, where he had his haunts.

It was an event the day when, after God knows what literary discussion, he abandoned Kalisaya, where he had become friends with Oscar Wilde, and started frequenting Bols, just across the street.

He could also sometimes be seen at Le Cardinal, where he stored some antiques in the office.

But the evening aperitif at the Napolitain became classic. He was there every evening. Three days before his death, he was still there.

He went to Vetzel, Tourtel, and Le Grand Café, too, but less regularly.

At *Le Journal*, he covered opening nights and literary obituaries of Académie members. For a while he was their theatre critic, after Catulle Mendès died.

Following *Les Nuits et les Ennuis*, he had another uncontested success with *L'Imitation de notre maître Napoléon*, striking a note well suited to those days when Stendhalian snobbery was de rigueur for literary men, with an anarcho-elegant and enigmatic form that Maurice Barrès had made fashionable – subtlety and Gongorism being far from unseductive features of this remarkable writer's work.

Cinq ans chez les sauvages, which contains the poignant story of Oscar Wilde's burial, still made a splash. But his later books (*L'Holocauste*, *Le Boulevard*, and *Le Forçat honoraire*) were successes only with the critics.

The new generations seemed to forget all about this man with his uncombed hair, his grey jacket, his wrinkled trousers, and his soft plush hat – the last of the boulevardiers.

Sem and Rouveyre and Cappiello: thanks to all the artists, Ernest la Jeunesse's figure is known far and wide. His was a very Parisian silhouette.

Ernest La Jeunesse belonged to the school of Jean de Tinan. His style is neological, and that is its weakness. But it is also moving, and that is its quality. Will this quality be enough to spare a few of his pages from oblivion? One might doubt it and suppose that, if we are to remember him, it is above all because he was the last of the boulevardiers.

The Quais and the Libraries

I go into the big libraries as seldom as I can. I prefer walking on the quais, that delectable public library.

This being said, I do sometimes visit the Bibliothèque Nationale or the Mazarine, and it was in the Bibliothèque du Musée Social, on rue Las-Cases, that I made the acquaintance of a remarkable reader who loved libraries.

'I remember', he told me, 'the profound weariness that used to come over me in the cities where I wandered, until, at last, to rest and return into the bosom of my family, I would go into a library.'

'Then you must be acquainted with quite a few of them.'

'They are central to my memories of the places I have travelled. I will pass over my long sojourns in the libraries of Paris. The admirable Bibliothèque Nationale, with its still-undiscovered treasures and its inkwells marked E. F. [Empire Français]. The Mazarine, where I got to know a few charming scholars: Léon Cahun, the author of first-rate novels that should have been more widely read; André Walckenear; and Albert Delavour. The first two are dead, and the third seems to have renounced both literature and libraries. Then, in the back of beyond, there's the Bibliothèque de l'Arsenal, which has one of the most precious poetry collections in the world. And finally the Bibliothèque de Sainte-Geneviève so beloved by Scandinavians.

'I think that, as far as light goes, the library in Lyon is one of the pleasantest. The sun shines in there better than in any of the libraries in Paris.

'At the little library in Nice I have read, with exquisite pleasure, Nostradamus's *Histoire de Provence* and researched the Saracens' Fraxinetum far from the music, plaster confetti, and floats of carnival.

'At the library in Quimper they have a collection of shells. One day when I was there a very fine gentleman came and examined them.

'"Are you the one who painted these baubles?" he asked the head librarian at the top of his voice. "No", the librarian replied calmly, "I am not, monsieur. Nature is the one who decorated these shells, with the most delicate colours." "You and I are never going to get on", the elegant visitor snapped back. "I leave you to it." And off he stalked.

'At Oxford there's a library (I don't remember which) where they burned all the works relating to sexuality. Remy de Gourmont's *La Physique de l'amour*, for example, and Ludwig Büchner's *Force and Matter*.

'At the university library in Jena, the academic senate decided to remove Heinrich Heine's works from the public reading room. They cannot be consulted except with special permission, in the stacks.

'In Cassel I kept hoping to see the ghost of Marquis de Luchet, the library's director in the late eighteenth century, who, according to the Germans, disorganised the holdings in a piecemeal fashion, shelving Wiquefort with the Church Fathers and inscribing barbarisms, such as *exeuropeana*, on the cards in the catalogue, which were found unacceptable not only by the Latinists of Cassel but those of Göttingen and Gotha. The latter made such a fuss that Luchet had to step down from his position.

'The library in Neuchâtel, Switzerland, has the finest view I've ever seen. Every last window overlooks the lake. An enchanting spot! The reading room is charming. It is decorated with portraits of Neuchâtel's more illustrious residents. And it's a very quiet place to do your reading since you almost never see anyone there. The administrator – and tradition dictates that this position is always held by a theologian – dozes at his desk. They have a copious collection of French books from the seventeenth and eighteenth centuries. And if someone asks for a book difficult to find, he is invited to go look for it himself. The library takes special pride in preserving some of Rousseau's manuscripts in a big yellow envelope, which is the only thing they hand over without complaint, they're so pleased with its very existence.

'At the library in St. Petersburg the *Mercure de France* could not be consulted in the reading room. The privileged went to read it in the area reserved for librarians. I saw some admirable Slavic manuscripts written on birch bark there. The library was open from 9:00 a.m. to 10:00 p.m. And in the reading room there were many poor students coming in to warm up. A real revolutionary hub. Repeated police raids, during which every reader would be required to show his passport, disturbed the otherwise studious atmosphere. You would see twelve-year-old girls in there reading Schopenhauer. Under the influence of Artsybashev's *Sanine*, you would also see elegant ladies reading the latest works of the French Symbolists.

'For a while Sanine's influence had very strange effects. Schoolboys and schoolgirls of fourteen to seventeen founded Sanineist societies. They would gather in a restaurant, where each boy or girl brought a candle-end and lit it. Then they would sing, and drink, and when the last candle went out, the orgy began.

'Just before the war there was a regrettable epidemic of suicides among young people that age.

'The library in Helsinki is very well stocked with French books, even the most recent ones.

'And on the Trans-Siberian railway the observation car contained, in addition to flowerpots and rocking chairs, a library of about five hundred volumes, more than half of which were French. They had books by Dumas père, George Sand, and Willy.

'Fort-de-France, Martinique, has a library – a big colonial villa built after the great fire of twenty or so years ago. When I was there, the curator was an old soldier depicted in that famous painting, *The Last Cartridges*. He was a charming scholar and did all the honours of his library himself – fetching books and so on. His name was Monsieur Saint-Félix, and if he is still among the living, I wish him good health.

'I once had the opportunity to visit the scientist Edison's library. I did not see *The Future Eve*, in which he figures as one of the characters. Perhaps he is not yet aware of Villiers de l'Isle-Adam's beautiful book. In fact, Edison's preferred reading was the fiction of Alexandre Dumas père. *The Three Musketeers* and *The Count of Monte Cristo* were on his nightstand.

'In New York, I had many long sessions at the Carnegie Library, an immense white marble building that, according to some of its patrons, is washed daily with black soap. The books are brought up by elevator. Each reader takes a number, and when his book arrives, an electric lamp comes on, illuminating the numeral corresponding to the one in the reader's hand. All day long, it sounds like a train station. A book takes about three minutes to arrive, and any delay is signalled by a bell. The workroom is immense, and in the ceiling, three coffers, which will someday have frescoes, for now contain grisaille clouds. Everyone and his cousin is admitted to the library. Before the war, all German books were acquired. Whereas acquisitions of French books were limited. Only famous French authors were purchased. When Henri de Régnier was elected to the Académie Française, all his works were ordered in a batch because the library didn't have even one. There is just one book there by Rachilde, *Le Meneur de Louves*, in a Russian translation, and in the catalogue you find the author's name in Russian, with a transliteration into the Latin alphabet followed by three question marks. Yet the library has subscribed to the *Mercure* for at least a decade. With no one checking, an average of 444 volumes are stolen every month. The most frequently stolen books are popular novels, which are therefore circulated in mimeograph. At the branches in working-class neighbourhoods, almost all the books are mimeographed. But the branch on Fourteenth Street (the Jewish neighbourhood) has an ample collection of books in Yiddish. In addition to the huge workroom I mentioned, there is a special room for music; a room for Semitic literatures; a room for technology; a room for U.S. patents; a room for the blind, where I saw a young girl reading Marguerite Audoux's *Marie-Claire* with her fingertips; a room for newspapers; and a room for typewriters accessible to the public. Finally, on the upper floor, there's a collection of paintings.

'And those are the libraries I have been to.'

'More than I have', I replied. And taking the Wanderer of Libraries by the arm, I did my best to change the topic of conversation.

On the quais one day I ran into Monsieur Ed. Cuénoud, a building manager in Montparnasse who devoted his leisure hours to bibliophily. He gave me an amusing little booklet he'd composed.

The booklet is illustrated by Carlègle. It is unknown and will no doubt eventually become legendary among bibliophiles on the hunt for imaginary catalogues.

The title is:

A CATALOGUE OF BOOKS FROM THE LIBRARY OF M. ED. C., *to be auctioned April 1st at the Salle des Bons-Enfants*.

And here are some items taken from this waggish catalogue:

ABEILARD. *Incomplete*, opened.
ALEXIS (P.). *Those We Do Not Marry*. Foxed.
ALLAIS (A.). *The Gang's Umbrella*. Bound in red percale.

ANGE BÉNIGNE. *Perdi, the Ladies' Tailor*. With notes and illustrations.

ARISTOPHANES. *The Frogs*. Marais Paper.*

AURIAC. *Fairground Theatre*. Watermarked paper.

BALZAC (H. DE). *The Wild Ass's Skin*. Reliquet idem.

BEAUMONT (A.). *The Handsome Colonel*. Perfectly preserved.

BOISGOBEY (F. DE). *Decapitated*. In 2 parts, damage to headband, red bottom edge.

BOREL (PÉTRUS). *Madame Putiphar*. Sold sub rosa.

CARLÈGLE AND GUÉNOUD. *Motorcar 217-U U*. Fine Whatman.

CERVANTES (MIGUEL DE). *Don Quixote*. Foolscap.

CLARETIE. *The Cigarette*. Rice paper.

COULON. *My Wife's Death*. Bound in half vellum.†

COURTELINE. *A Serious Client*. Rare, much sought-after.

DUBUT DE LAFORÊT. *The Dodderer*. Quite faded.

DUFFERIN (LORD). *Letters Written in the Polar*

---

* 'Papier du Marais' indicates a high-quality paper; taken literally, it means 'paper from the marsh'.

† *Chagrin*, in French, means both grief and untanned leather (vellum).

Regions. Glossy paper.

DUMAS (A.). *Napoleon*. A large volume.

DUMAS FILS (A.). *The Friend of Women*. Completely o.p.

DUMAS FILS (A.). *Monsieur Alphonse*. Green spine.

FLEURIOT (Z.). *A Dried Fruit*. Awarded a prize by the Académie française.

GAIGNET. *Bossuet*. Grand-Aigle paper.*

GAZIER. *Port-Royal of the Fields*. Jansenist binding.

GRANDMOUGIN. *The Strongbox*. Opens with a key.

GRAYE. (TH. DE). *The Parvenu*. With half title.

GUIMBAIL. *The Morphine Addicts*. Stippled.

HAUPTMANN. *The Weavers*. Clothbound.

HAVARD (H.). *Amsterdam and Venice*. Small capitals.

HERVILLY (E. D'). *Mal aux cheveaux*. A lovely fig.

KARR (A.). *The Wasps*. Raised bands.

KOCK (P. DE). *A Compendium of Famous Cuckolds*. With transparent horn-plate.

LA FONTAINE. *Hans Carvel's Ring*. On the Index.

---

* *Grand-Aigle*, literally 'Great Eagle', is a French paper format. Bossuet, the Bishop of Meaux, was nicknamed the Eagle of Meaux.

LA FONTAINE. *The Heron and the Fish*. Water-stained.

MAETERLINCK. *The Treasure of the Humble*. Chipped.

MAINDRON. *Weapons*. Steel engravings.

MATTEY. *The Thousand-Franc Note*. Very rare.

MAURY (L.). *Abd-el-Aziz*. Crushed Morocco.

MONTBART (G.). *The Melon*. Uncut.

REMUSAT (P. DE). *Monsieur Thiers*. A small volume.

THIERRY (G.-A.). *The Audacious Captain*. Limp binding.

VIGNY. *Cinq-Mars*. Missing headband.

VILMORIN. *Bulbs*. Printed on onionskin.

VOLTAIRE. *The Age of Louis XIV*. Magnificent illustrations of all kinds, etc., etc.

Quite a curious bibliographical bauble.

I used to see Monsieur Ed. Guénoud on the quais now and then. He died not long ago, and whenever I pass the bouquinistes' boxes by the Institute, I recall the singular silhouette of this manager, who, in his waggish bibliography, rivalled Rabelais and Remy de Gourmont, and never failed to take a stroll along the quais before nightfall.

Isn't that the most delightful walk you can take in Paris? It isn't too much, if you have the time, to devote a whole afternoon to strolling from the Gare d'Orsay to the Pont Saint-Michel. Probably there's no walk in the world more beautiful, or more pleasant.

The Convent on rue de Douai

Whenever I pass the corner of rue de Douai and Place Clichy, where today there's a school and, before the division, there used to be a convent where my first book, *L'Enchanteur pourrissant*, was printed, my thoughts turn to Monsieur Paul Birault.

As everyone knows, Birault once encouraged the formation of a committee of delegates – most of them senators – who campaigned to erect a statue to a made-up demagogue called Hégésippe Simon. The mastermind behind this hoax revealed all the delicious details in *L'Éclair*, and the hoaxer became more famous than the coiners of a word that Voltaire disparaged, who so maliciously bamboozled silly old Poinsinet, who eventually drowned himself in the Guadalquivir. Unlike the so-called Boronali hoax, which fooled no one, Birault pulled the wool over the eyes of all the parliamentarians he had chosen as his victims. Not one of these men laughed at the epigraph, taken from the purported works of Hégésippe Simon, 'the forefather of Democracy', which adorned a letter urging them to help raise a monument in the birthplace of this great man – born in more cities than Homer.

'When the sun rises, darkness disappears.' Such was the phrase Paul Birault attributed to Hégésippe Simon. It sums up the better part of the eloquence men are so hungry to hear – the eloquence that, with the help of the phonograph, has the brightest future ahead of it.

The second coming of Caillot-Duval,* who also did their work through the post, Monsieur Birault found himself described in the newspapers as 'our distinguished colleague'. He would have needed to push just a little for the title of 'eminent', and if eventually he felt like entering the Académie française, he would simply have had to insert himself in certain salons, where, being a witty man, he would have thrived.

---

* Caillot-Duval is the pseudonym of two young aristocrats who perpetrated epistolary hoaxes in the late eighteenth century, playing to and with the vanity of various public figures.

I first met Monsieur Birault in 1910, when he did me the honour of printing my first book. At that time, Birault had an established printshop in the convent at the end of rue de Douai, at the corner of Place Clichy. He had already printed my first preface to a catalogue for the first exhibition of the painter Georges Braque, the well-known cubist, illustrious accordion player, redesigner of costumes (long before the Delaunays), and jig dancer emeritus, for I think the problems of painting led him to give up dancing back in 1915, when dancing was all the rage. It was Birault's friendship with the painter Kees van Dongen that made him then, as he still is today, the preferred printer of the man who published the Braque catalogue and my own first book.*

It was agreed that I would oversee the printing with the help of the book's illustrator, my friend André Derain, who had made the most beautiful modern woodcuts I've ever seen.

One sunny morning the publisher, André Derain, and I went over to the convent on rue de Douai, where we met Monsieur Birault. He was then a small, expressionless man with pinched, sickly features. I

---

* Daniel-Henry Kahnweiler.

imagined that he was unsatisfied with his position as a small-time printer. He had published songs that had been sung in concerts, as he showed us. He loved puns, and when I saw him again later, he told me the details of several hoaxes he had concocted; I think he had even put one into action, but I no longer quite remember. It had something to do with the metro. He had his hands full with his printshop until his wife, an intelligent and industrious woman, shouldered the lion's share of the labour. By then he was working nights at a major newspaper.

I got to know Monsieur Birault away from his workplace, too, and had dinner at his home. I must say he treated me very well. I have noticed that people who know how to eat are rarely fools. One hundred and four copies of *L'Enchanteur pourrissant* were printed – and well printed – by Monsieur Paul Birault.

Today this book is almost famous. Most of the plates that illustrate it have been reproduced in art magazines the world over. I think that Monsieur Birault's work as a printer may be among the only contemporary French publications that owe nothing to foreign styles and have had an influence on printing abroad. Those one hundred and four small quartos with the scallop shell mark, designed by André Derain, salvaged the typographical reputation of France at a time when the French were all cooing over the typography of Germany, England, Belgium, and Holland. No one in France has said a word about this, and for me to find an excuse to do so, my printer had to become a famous hoaxer.

Being a truly intelligent man, Monsieur Birault was free of vanity. I am sure that, even after he became famous, he was as modest as ever, and that all the gourmets of the Club des Cent found him as knowledgeable as they were themselves, without a trace of pride when it came to matters of the mouth.

After *L'Enchanteur pourrissant* and before he invented the Forefather of Democracy, I happened to run into Monsieur Birault again, when he was already a well-established journalist. He covered aviation for *Paris-Journal*, was echoer-in-chief * at *La France*, head of news at *L'Opinion*, columnist at *L'Éclair*, and still involved with his shop, where Max Jacob's books were still being printed.

---

* 'Chef des échos' is a term taken from Guy de Maupassant's *Bel-Ami*, for a newspaper editor who contrives to shape public opinion.

He stayed in the convent on rue de Douai until the end – until the moment of demolition. Canny as he was, he contrived, I believe, to have himself evicted, and the monastery was already being demolished, the dancing Negroes had been having a bash for some time, even as Monsieur Birault, with his little wife and child, went on gathering every evening under the family lamp, in the cell that served as their dining room.

Having made his name in the world of journalists as a hoaxer, Paul Birault remained well known in the new literary circles as a printer.

In the little shop on rue Tardieu where he moved after leaving rue de Douai, Pierre Reverdy and Philippe Soupault's first chapbooks were printed, as well as a some of the shape-poems from my collection *Calligrammes*. The books printed by Paul Birault will live on in the libraries of bibliophiles.

During the war he was the wittiest of contributors to the *Bulletin des Armées de la République*. He died in 1918, just as the Berthas and the Gothas were making a sinister noise.

The Bouillon Michel Pons

Not long before the war I met Monsieur Michel
Pons – the restaurateur-poet who, in an academic
election, had the vote of Maurice Barrès – and he
invited me to come visit him. A few days later I
turned up at the Bouillon Michel Pons, on rue des
Moulins, at about five o'clock in the afternoon.

A white-haired woman with a very pleasant face
told me the boss was upstairs, and I climbed up
some narrow spiral steps.

In a low-ceilinged room lighted by a gas lamp,
with his friend, the shoemaker-philosopher André
Gayet, Michel Pons sat pasting up newspaper clippings concerning his latest book of verse, *Les
Chants d'un déraciné*.

Monsieur Pons is a man in the prime of life; he
is dark-haired, not very tall, but broad-shouldered
and firmly planted on his legs. He is easily excited,

even quicker to laugh, and always illustrates his stories with pugilistic gestures.

His friend the shoemaker-philosopher makes a striking contrast. He is very tall and thin, which, despite his white hair, makes him look quite young. His expression is tranquil. A rather pronounced squint makes him seem distant and mysterious. He rarely speaks, and when he does what comes out is commonsense. When he listens, you can see him calculating the worth of what he hears, constantly trying to give his interlocutor the benefit of the doubt. His very tidy clothes are those of a crafts-man, but his height and posture give them real elegance. Right off the bat he reminded me of a friend of mine whom he greatly resembled, René Dalize, my first schoolfriend.

After the introductions, my two colleagues and I looked over the clippings that Michel Pons had just pasted up. Then I looked over some others he had received earlier. There were quite a few.

Nothing excites curiosity so much as a professional man with intellectual interests. The fact that Michel Pons combines the qualities of a poet and a restaura-teur has been a source of astonishment as far away as Australia. He has been interviewed more frequently than Edmond Rostand, and his photograph has been published almost as often as that of a great actress.

I could see that Michel Pons and André Gayet, who set great store by publicity, were alert to any opportunity to get more of it.

'When one believes that, through one's writings, one is rendering service to men', the shoemaker-philosopher said, 'isn't it only right to do whatever one can to reach them?'

Later, a tall, very alert and pleasant-looking red-head, who looked like Hop-o'-my-Thumb's eldest brother, came in and threw his arms around André Gayet, kissing him on both cheeks. It was his son, who is an apprentice pastry chef.

'He wants to be a chef', said the philosopher, 'but I thought first he should learn pastry-making... I know people in kitchens, and if he could become a great cook, like Carême or Escoffier, it would certainly be an enviable lot.'

I understood that this good and quite reasonable man, instead of pushing his son out of his condition, wished to give him the means to reach an important position within it.

As for Michel Pons, he shelved the fate of his own new book to quiz his friend, asking weather he'd served his book, *La Théorie du succès*, to various useful people. He then gave advice on the steps to be taken, in the course of which I learned that, after personally handling *La Théorie's* publication, he had already done a good deal to help it along, having written several praiseful reviews.

And when I left these two friends, holding *Les Chants d'un déraciné* under one arm, I opened *La Théorie du succès* and began humming a Provençal song quoted by Mistral:

> At the fountain in Nîmes
> There is a cobbler
> Who sings all day long
> As he makes his shoes.
> And if he is singing still
> It is not for us;
> He is singing for his beloved
> Beside him.

Since the war, I have stopped in to say hello to Maurice Barrès' friend again. Monsieur Pons has aged a little, but he still loves poetry and good bourgeois cuisine. His restaurant does a good business, and you can still sometimes see, in the crowd of silly girls, a few poets and journalists.

An Obscure Napoleonic Museum

If you ever go down rue de Poissy, stop at number 14 and try to visit the little Napoleonic museum there.

Before the war, this museum had its own publication, called the *Journal du Musée*.

I don't know if there was a more curious gazette in France, or even the whole world, than the *Journal du Musée*. Publication: bimonthly, on the 1st and 15th. Address: 14, rue de Poissy. Subscription: 3 francs a year. Printed in purple using a mimeograph machine, it ran in three columns on two pages. This sheet was published by a ten-year-old child as an advertising organ for the museum he founded, dedicated to Napoleon.

This Napoleonic museum is not well known. It contains some interesting and valuable items collected by the boy himself. Booksellers, antiques dealers, and enthusiasts, charmed by the child's initiative, have added to the riches of this unforeseeable institution with donations. The Journal's subscribers were numerous, I was told, and more often than not the newspaper appeared very regularly. It went for ten centimes an issue.

I have a copy of this peculiar paper. The lead article, 'The Continuation of a Life of Napoleon', by G. Ducoudray, runs for a column and a half. After that, the Museum section provides some important information:

> The museum has reopened. No one would recognise it. Great changes have taken place. Many donations have enriched the museum, among them donations from Messrs. Thiébaut and Mattei.

A serialized tale by Alphonse Daudet livens up the *Journal du Musée* in a highly literary way, and what space remains is given over to wit and imagination. Here are some riddles:

> Which café do speculators frequent?
> Which café do clean people frequent?
> Which café do watchmakers frequent?

Who crosses the river without getting wet?
How many sides does a square pâté have?

And an epigram:

Monsieur Binet, though opulently rich,
Lacks the comfort and ease craved today.
As for me, if I had his affluence,
I would certainly do things my way.

I don't believe the ten-year-old child was the author. In any case, all this gave the *Journal du Musée* an irreverence that could not be farther from the contemporary prudishness. The last column contains 'Answers to the questions posed in the previous issue' and 'The Answer to the Rebus': 'Help yourself, and Heaven will help you.' Only three people solved it: Messrs. Grund, Henri Guérard, and Mattei.

One final announcement informs us that 'Due to an accident during the printing process, this issue was published 15 days late. We apologise to our readers for the inconvenience.'

No director's name or mention of a printer legalises the publication of this little paper, one of whose chief peculiarities – the age of its director and editor-in-chief – is destined to disappear as, for us as for him, the years go by.

I have known other children who amused themselves publishing newspapers. But they were always handwritten, a single copy, passed around from hand to hand at school. I particularly remember one of these pamphlets, which was calligraphed in different coloured inks: black, purple, green, blue, yellow, and red. It was to appear every week, and the subscription was to be paid in sweets – liquorice, brown sugar, cans of coconut milk, etc. – but there was no second issue.

A girl of ten, who is now nearly a young woman, joined forces with a boy of seven to publish a paper. She collected subscriptions for the sum of thirty francs, giving five to the little boy and using the rest to buy herself some chocolate. This anticipatory triumph – as it was, for her – completely satisfied her need for activity. So it is that premature success almost always leads to decadence in poets and artists of all kinds.

Monsieur Vollard's Cellar

Near the boulevard, at 8, rue Laffitte, there was a shop before the war – a real mare's nest, in which the canvases of contemporary painters were all piled up and dust reigned supreme.

Since the war, the shop has been shuttered. Monsieur Vollard no doubt has given up his business to devote himself entirely to his writerly imagination and the composition of his memoirs, which will touch on the painters and authors he has known. He will not forget to say something about his cellar, which was well known from 1900 until around 1908, when he announced to me that he was giving up eating there because it had gotten too damp.

Everyone has heard of this illustrious hypogeum. It was even considered fashionable for a while to be invited there for lunch or dinner. I personally was present at some of these meals. The cellar, with its tiles and all-white walls, felt like a little monasic refectory.

The cuisine was simple but delicious, the dishes prepared according to the principles of old French cookery still current in the colonies – dishes cooked for a long time, over low heat, livened up with exotic seasonings.

Among the guests at these underground feasts were, first and foremost, a great many pretty women, followed by Monsieur Léon Dierx, the prince of poets; Monsieur Forain, the prince of artists; Alfred Jarry, Odilon Redon, Maurice Denis, Maurice De Vlaminck, José-Maria Sert, Vuillard, Bonnard, K.X. Roussel, Aristide Maillol, Picasso, Émile Bernard, Derain, Marius-Ary Leblond, Claude Terrasse, etc., etc.

Bonnard painted a picture of the cellar, and if memory serves, you can make out Odilon Redon in it.

Léon Dierx was present at almost all of these meals. I got to know him in that cellar. His eyesight was already failing. Those who saw him only in the street or at poetic ceremonies, where he presided with such serene majesty, have no idea how jolly the old poet could be.

His good mood faded only when his poems were recited, and there was almost inevitably one young person or another who suddenly got up and lobbed a poem of his at his head.

One evening Madame Berthe Raynold was the culprit, and she recited it so well that the prince of poets didn't mind. But then one of the guests, who had just been claiming to know Paris and contemporary poetry like the back of his hand, asked loudly: 'Is that Lamartine or Victor Hugo?' Monsieur Vollard had to tell twenty stories about the natives of Zanzibar before Monsieur Dierx resolved to smile again.

Léon Dierx used to love telling stories about his time working for the government. He would go about his work, thinking of lines all the while. Once he had to write to a sub-prefectural archivist, and instead of 'Monsieur Archivist', he wrote 'Monsieur Anarchist', which caused a great scandal in the sub-prefecture.

Léon Dierx's favorite painters were Corot, Monticelli, and Forain.

As we were leaving Monsieur Vollard's cellar one evening, the prince of poets invited me to come see him at his home in Batignolles, where he gave me a very warm welcome.

On the walls, Monticelli's paintings of the *Decameron* hung beside Forain's sketches, and the ancient, variegated figures of the former seemed to combine with the modern, spiritual silhouettes of the other to form a strange and lyrical court for this nearly blind prince of the aristocratic Republic of Letters.

A Parnassian, he was indulgent toward poets of all schools (as parties are called in the land of the poets).

'Any theory can be good', he said, 'but the work itself is the only thing that matters.'

He was reserved when he spoke of contemporary literature, but if he happened to utter the name Moréas, his voice rose, and one supposed that a secret preference would have dictated his choice, if sovereigns were obliged to choose.

He once said to me: 'Our age of prose and science has known the most lyrical poets. Their lives and adventures form the strangest part of the history of our time.

'Gérard de Nerval killed himself to escape the miseries of existence, and the mystery surrounding his death has not yet been explained.

'Baudelaire died mad – Baudelaire, whose life we know so little about, despite the biographers and the editors of letters. Everyone has gone on about his vices and mistresses. But now they say Nadar, in his *Memoirs*, goes to great lengths to demonstrate that Baudelaire died a virgin.

'Even as we speak, a poet of the first order – a mad poet – is wandering the world... Germain Nouveau left the high school where he was teaching drawing one day and became a beggar, following the example of Saint Benedict Labre. He went away to Italy, where he painted and lived off the sales of his paintings. Now he walks the pilgrimage routes. I hear that he has been to Brussels, Lourdes, Africa. But "mad" is going too far. Germain Nouveau is conscious of his condition. He's a mystic. He doesn't want to be called a "Madman" or a "lyrical Poverello". The only word he wants applied to him is "Insane".

'Some friends have had his poems published. Having renounced his own name, the author of them is listed, rather mystically, as P.N. Humilis, a kind of religious name. But his humility would be offended by this publication, if he knew it existed.'

Léon Dierx relit his meerschaum pipe. He shook his handsome head with its long white hair.

'Germain Nouveau can still paint', he said, 'I can't anymore. My eyesight keeps getting worse. I'm almost blind. I can no longer read the books people send me. In the old days, I used to pass the time painting. I know of no life happier than that of a landscape painter...'

This prince from the islands has been succeeded by another poet prince, Paul Fort, who is only a little older than us.

The *Grand Almanach illustré* came together in the rue Laffitte cellar. Everyone knows Alfred Jarry wrote the text, Bonnard did the illustrations, and Claude Terrasse composed the music. As for the song, it's by Monsieur Ambroise Vollard. Everyone knows this, and yet no one ever seems to mention that the *Grand Almanach illustré* was published without the names of the authors or the publisher.

The night he dreamed up almost everything in this work worthy of Rabelais, Jarry terrified everyone who didn't know him by asking, after dinner, for the pickle jar, from which he ate like a glutton.

Many former guests will mourn this picturesque corner of Paris and the white vault of that cellar where, a stone's throw from the boulevards, you could enjoy some peace and quiet, without a single painting on the walls.